Because
I SAID SO...
a biblical study of obedience
JUNIOR

TABLE OF CONTENTS

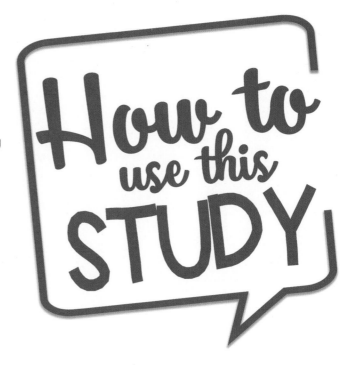

The study is written with the mid to late elementary school student in mind. Such a student should be fairly comfortable completing this study on his/her own during Bible time, quiet time or whatever works for your family. It is assumed that the student has some Bible knowledge, so if your child has limited knowledge, you might need to work together.

Of course, this study would be a perfect family study with mom/dad reading aloud to children who are not yet proficient readers!

Also, if your child is uncomfortable with all the writing, I would suggest that you allow him/her to answer the questions verbally. The point of the study is not to test his/her writing skills, but to help him/her grow in Christ!

As written, the study spans about 3-4 weeks for about 20-35 minutes a day, but can be broken up into whatever chunks work best for your family. No need to stress about it. Simply do one page each time you have the opportunity to work in the study. It will be fine if you skip a few days in between!

Included at the end of the study is a bonus hymn study on the beloved hymn, Trust and Obey. This could be used at the beginning, all throughout the study or at the end. It's completely up to you!

A note about translation: I have purposely not included the specific quoting of most scripture so that you are free to use the translation you prefer. However, it may be important to note that I use the KJV and ESV versions to study and I wrote this study using those resources. If a particular question doesn't make sense, you might try the KJV or ESV version for clarification.

Helpful websites:
A great bible dictionary: http://www.thekingsbible.com/BibleDictionary.aspx

Find hymn info at www.hymnary.org

WHAT DOES IT MEAN TO OBEY?

Look up the biblical definition for "obey" and write it below.

OBEY _____

_____

_____

Before we study what the Bible says about obedience, write or draw what you think it means to obey.

How do you obey?

Who do you obey?

Why do you obey?

OBEY WITHOUT DELAY

God has given us very specific instructions in His Word about HOW we should obey him. Let's look at the first one. Read **Jonah 1:1-17**. What did God ask Jonah to do? v.2

_____

_____

_____

_____

_____

_____

What did Jonah do? v.3

_____

_____

_____

_____

_____

_____

_____

Because Jonah disobeyed, there were 2 consequences. Write or draw your answers in the boxes. (See v. 4 and v. 17)

CONSEQUENCE 1

CONSEQUENCE 2

What did Jonah do next? (Read **Jonah 2:1-10**)

_____

_____

God was merciful with Jonah and gave him a second chance.

Read **Jonah 3:1-3**. Did Jonah obey God right away this time?

_____

Because of Jonah's obedience, what happened to the people of Nineveh? (**Jonah 3:6-10**)

_____

_____

Journal ABOUT IT Write about a time when you didn't obey right away. Ask God to forgive you for being disobedient.

_____

_____

_____

_____

_____

_____

_____

POWER TRUTH
God desires that we obey without delay.

OBEY COMPLETELY

Let's read about Israel's first king, Saul, in **I Samuel 15:1-9**. God asked King Saul to do two things in verse 3. Name them.

1. _____ Amalek and

2. _____ everything they have.

What did Saul do in verses 4-8?

_____

If we aren't careful, we would think that Saul obeyed God, right? But look at verse 9. Did Saul obey completely? ☐YES ☐NO

Read verses 10-21. In verse 21, Samuel confronts Saul about keeping the spoil. What excuse does Saul give?

_____

_____

On the surface it looks like Saul had a good reason to disobey God, right? Have you ever had a time when you disobeyed God or your parents because you thought it seemed like a good reason? What happened?

_____

_____

_____

_____

God didn't think it was a good reason. What does God say in verse 22?

To OBEY is _____ than sacrifice.

In verse 23, what is the consequence that God gives King Saul for not obeying Him completely?

_____

Journal ABOUT IT Write about a time when you obeyed, but not completely. For example, you cleaned your room, but hid a pile of dirty clothes under your bed. Pray and ask God to forgive you for being disobedient by not obeying completely.

_____
_____
_____
_____
_____
_____
_____
_____
_____
_____

POWER TRUTH
God desires that we obey completely.

© NOT CONSUMED 2017

OBEY WITHOUT QUESTION

Sometimes God (or our parents) ask us to do things that seem crazy or make no sense. Right away I think of two people in the Bible who experienced this. Read **Genesis 6:9-22.** What did God ask Noah to do? (v. 14)

_____

The people had never seen a flood. They surely thought Noah was crazy! But look at verse 22. What does it say that Noah did?

_____

Look at that verse again. Did he ask God why? Did he question God's thinking?

_____

Let's look at another man who obeyed God. Read **Genesis 12:1-9.** What did God ask Abram to do? (v.1)

What important information was Abram lacking? (See **Hebrews 11:8**)

_____

What did Abram do? (v.4)

_____

_____

Journal ABOUT IT   Both Noah and Abram obeyed God without question! They didn't demand an explanation or more details about what God was going to do! They were both blessed for their obedience to God and listed in Hebrews as men of great faith. Write about a time when you had to obey someone without knowing why or without knowing some of the details. Did you do it without question, like Abram and Noah? Pray and ask God to forgive you if you did question.

_____

_____

_____

_____

_____

_____

_____

_____

POWER TRUTH
God desires that we obey without question.

OBEY JOYFULLY

Read **Numbers 20:2-13.** What problem does Moses have and what does God tell him to do about it? (v2 and v8)

_____

_____

What does Moses do in verse 11?

What does Moses do in verse 11?

On the surface it looks like Moses has done a great job obeying God, but what does God say to him in verse 12?

_____

_____

Did Moses do exactly what God told him to do? ☐YES ☐NO
What was the problem? (Read verses 10-11 again and pay close attention to Moses' attitude.)

I bet you have done what Moses did. Can you think of a time when you obeyed but did so while stomping your feet, slamming a door, throwing something and/or yelling mean things at your siblings? Write about it.

_____

_____

_____

God desires that we obey joyfully. And he considered Moses' behavior an act of disobedience. Why? (see v. 12)

_____

_____

We are going to look more at this point, but be sure you don't miss that **God called Moses' disobedience UNBELIEF!** When we refuse to willingly submit in joyful obedience, we are telling God that we don't trust Him and we don't believe Him. Ouch!

Journal ABOUT IT

Write out a prayer right now asking God to forgive you for all the times that you didn't obey joyfully.

_____

_____

_____

_____

_____

_____

_____

POWER TRUTH
God desires that we obey joyfully.

HOW DO
WE OBEY?

God desires that we obey

_____

God desires that we obey

_____

God desires that we obey

_____

God desires that we obey

_____

WEEK2

11

OBEDIENCE SHOWS YOU BELIEVE

Last week we talked about HOW we should obey. This week we will focus on WHY we should obey. It's not a bad thing to obey "because God (or mom) said so," but there is much more to it than that. Let's dig in!

You probably know that God promised Sarah and Abraham a son, even though they were very old. In **Genesis 21** this promised son, Isaac, is born. This makes it hard to believe that God would ask Abraham to do what he did in **Genesis 22**. Let's check it out.

Read **Genesis 22:1-2**. What did God ask Abraham to do?

Now read verses 3-14. Did Abraham obey? _____

Why do you think God tested Abraham in this way? (see **Hebrews 11:17-19**)

Hebrews 11:17-19 shows us that God saw Abraham's obedience as FAITH. God had no intention of harming Isaac. God wanted Abraham to show that he truly believed, by obeying what God had commanded him.

God takes our unbelief very seriously. Write out **Hebrews 11:6**.

_____

_____

_____

_____

Write a prayer to God asking Him to forgive you for not believing Him enough to obey.

_____

_____

_____

_____

_____

_____

_____

_____

_____

POWER TRUTH

Obedience shows you believe.

OBEDIENCE SHOWS LOVE

Jesus himself told us exactly why we should obey. Let's read it in **John 14:15**. Then write the verse below.

_____

_____

_____

When did Jesus say we should obey? Sometimes? If we want to? When it seems good? Read **John 14:15** again and write your answer.

_____

Throughout His time on earth, Jesus did many things to obey God. Read about one of them in **Philippians 2:8**. What did Jesus do?

_____

_____

Now, remind yourself again. Why did Jesus die on the cross?

Because God so _____ the world (John 3:16) that He gave His son for the forgiveness of our

_____.

If He hadn't died on the cross, what would happen to us? **(Romans 6:23)**

_____

Journal ABOUT IT

Jesus' obedience on the cross showed the ultimate love, both to us and to God. How awesome is that? Write a prayer to Him thanking Him for loving us that much!

_____

_____

_____

_____

_____

In what ways have you shown love to God or your parents through obedience this week?

_____

_____

_____

_____

_____

_____

_____

_____

_____

POWER TRUTH

Obedience shows you love.

OBEDIENCE IS A WITNESS TO OTHERS

You've probably heard the story of Shadrach, Meshach, and Abednego. Let's take another look at it and find out what benefit their obedience had.

Read **Daniel 3:1-30**. What did the King expect all of the people in his kingdom to do? v.1 and v. 4-5

What was the punishment for those who did not worship the golden idol? v. 6

_____

Did Shadrach, Meshach, and Abednego obey the king and bow down to the idol? v. 12

☐ YES   ☐ NO

Naturally, this made King Nebuchadnezzar very angry. What reason did the friends give for not bowing down? v.16-18

_____

It took a lot of courage for them to disobey the king in order to obey God. They were indeed thrown into the fiery furnace. BUT, there was an amazing benefit of this brave act. What was it? v. 28-29

_____

_____

_____

Journal ABOUT IT

Tell about a time when you made a hard choice to obey God that turned out to be a good example or witness to those around you. Or write a prayer asking God to help you obey Him so that you can be a better witness for Him.

_____

_____

_____

_____

_____

_____

_____

_____

Romans 1:5 reminds us that our obedience is a witness. Write it here.

POWER TRUTH

Obedience is a witness to others.

OBEDIENCE BRINGS
BLESSING

If you ask someone why you should obey God, chances are they will tell you that obedience to God brings blessing in your life. Let's see what the Bible says about that.

Read **Genesis 22:18**. How did God bless Abraham for obeying?

_____

How about Shadrach, Meshach, and Abednego? What blessing did they receive in **Daniel 3:30?**

_____

Read **Genesis 9:1**. What was the result of Noah's obedience to God?

_____

The Bible is full of stories where people obeyed God and God rewarded them richly. Of course, this is a good reason to obey God, but let us not be so eager to get blessing that we forget the reasons we have already learned for obeying God. List them here.

Obedience _____

Obedience _____

Obedience _____

Obeying God's Word really is a blessing.

Write **Luke 11:28**.

_____

_____

This doesn't necessarily mean that God will give us a long life on earth, lots of money or a large family if we obey Him. But, He does promise to bless us. What is the most important blessing that God promises to us? See **James 1:12.**

_____

_____

Write a prayer to God thanking Him for the gracious gift of eternal life. Be sure to ask Him to forgive you for any disobedience today or this week.

_____

_____

_____

_____

_____

_____

POWER TRUTH

Obedience brings blessing.

WHY SHOULD WE OBEY?

Obedience

_____

Obedience

_____

Obedience

_____

Obedience

_____

WEEK 3

WHO SHOULD WE OBEY?

In the last two weeks we've looked at HOW we should obey God and WHY we should obey God. No doubt, you have made up your mind to obey God.

But did you realize that God commands us to obey more than just Him? Let's read **Ephesians 6:1** and write it below.

_____

_____

_____

_____

It's pretty neat that this was the first commandment with a promise. Write that promise here. (v. 3)

God has very intentionally put your parents in authority over you. It's a wonderful way that He is protecting you and blessing you. Fill in the blanks from what you have learned the past two weeks.

We obey our parents because it shows that

we _____ God, it shows them that

we _____ them,

and it's a _____ to others.

Have you ever thought about it that way before? _____

Journal ABOUT IT Write a prayer asking God to forgive you for all of the times that you have disobeyed your parents showing unbelieving, unloving, and unchristian behavior.

_____

_____

_____

_____

_____

_____

_____

_____

_____

_____

_____

_____

_____

_____

OBEYING OTHERS

Inside our homes, we are commanded to obey our parents. But since we don't just stay inside our homes all day, there are others that we might need to obey.

Read **Hebrews 13:17**. Write the verse below.

_____

_____

_____

_____

WHO SHOULD WE OBEY?

Underline the word in the verse on that last page that tells who you are supposed to obey. The Bible says we are to obey our leaders, or those who have rule over us. Who do you think that includes?

Circle all that apply.

mom/dad   uncle/aunt

school teachers   pastor

the president   babysitter

police officers   grandparents

sunday school teachers

Hopefully you circled them all. Each one of those people have been placed over you as an authority. Which leads to an important question:

What if your leader isn't following God?

Do you still obey?

Think back to the stories in Daniel. Multiple times the king asked them to do something against God's word such as eat the king's meat and bow down to his idols. Even though the boys were pretty young, they still understood the keys to obedience. Read **Daniel 3:16-17** again. Why did Shadrach, Meshach and Abednego refuse to bow to the idol?

_____

_____

_____

_____

_____

Do you think they were right? The end of the story tells us that God approved of their choice. They were saved from that fire and their testimony caused the king to order that everyone was to worship God. It's important to notice one thing, though. They didn't disobey because the king didn't believe in God. They disobeyed the king ONLY when he asked them to do something that was against God's word. And that is the key for us, too.

Our obedience to nonbelievers is a testimony of our obedience to God, as long as they don't ask us to go against God. This means that if the government makes a law which says we can't speed, we need to obey it. Not because they are godly, but because they are our authority.

Journal ABOUT IT

Write some reasons that you might not obey someone and discuss these with your parents or pastor. Whenever you are in doubt, always seek wise godly counsel from mom/dad or pastor.

_____

_____

_____

_____

_____

_____

_____

_____

_____

_____

_____

_____

_____

_____

We've learned a lot about obedience. Have you noticed over the past few weeks how often you are guilty of disobeying? You probably did and there is a reason for that.

Read **Romans 3:23.** Why do we keep messing up, even when we try so hard?

_____

Remember that **if we could have kept all of God's laws perfectly, then Jesus would not have had to die for us!**

Paul had the same problem in **Romans 7:15**. While he wanted to do right, what did he end up doing? (see the last half of the verse)

Believe it or not, your mom and dad struggle with this, too. We are all guilty of disobeying God. Does that mean we should just stop trying to please God? Of course not! **We want to obey God, so we must not give up!**

Think of a time recently when you blew it - either God or your parents or even another leader asked you to do something and you disobeyed. Write about that time below.

_____

_____

_____

_____

_____

_____

_____

_____

_____

Read **I Corinthians 10:13**. The Bible tells us here that God will not let us be tempted beyond what we can bear. It also says that when we are tempted, God will give us what?

_____

Let's look at the story of when Jesus was tempted to disobey God. Read **Matthew 4:1-11**. What did Jesus use to keep Himself from sinning?

_____

Memorizing God's Word is a great way to help us obey. Another way is prayer. Write **Isaiah 65:24** below.

_____

_____

_____

Journal ABOUT IT

If you ask, God will help you obey. Let's do that right now. Write a prayer to God asking Him to help you obey when it seems difficult like that time that you wrote about above.

_____

_____

_____

_____

_____

_____

_____

_____

BEFORE WE SAY GOODBYE

James 1:22 reminds us that we should be doers of the Word and not just hearers. We've learned a lot about what obedience really looks like and about why we should want to obey. Take some time today and write a letter to God telling Him all that you learned, why you WANT to obey Him and how you will use that to help you every day from now on!

Journal ABOUT IT

_____

_____

_____

_____

_____

_____

_____

_____

_____

_____

_____

_____

_____

_____

_____

_____

_____

_____

Because I Said So

Appendix

TRUST AND OBEY
THE STORY

The tune for this beloved hymn was written by Daniel B. Towner, a beloved vocalist and music teacher.

In 1885, during one of Mr. Moody's revival meetings, a young man gave a testimony saying, " I am not quite sure-but I am going to trust, and I am going to obey."

Dr. Towner wrote those words down and sent them back to a Presbyterian minister, Rev. J.H. Sammis. The Reverend composed the words into a poem and sent it back to Dr. Towner to write the music. He wrote the hymn as we know it today.

In 1893, Dr. Towner became head of the music department at Moody Bible Institute. There he trained hundreds of young people to lead worship and minister to the Lord through music. He wrote many other beloved hymns such as "At Calvary" and "Grace Greater Than All Our Sins." He also compiled 14 hymnbooks and wrote several textbooks.

HYMN STUDY NOTES

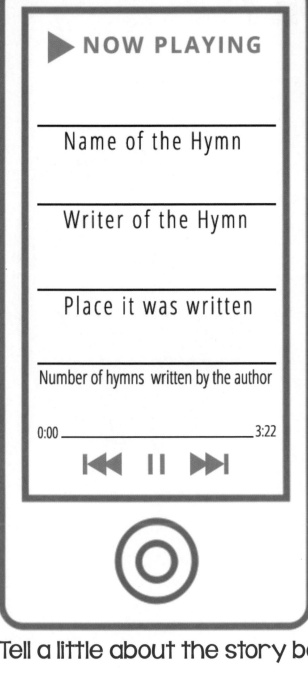

► NOW PLAYING

_____
Name of the Hymn

_____
Writer of the Hymn

_____
Place it was written

_____
Number of hymns written by the author

0:00 _____ 3:22

⏮ ⏸ ⏭

Some facts about the author:

_____
_____
_____
_____
_____
_____
_____

Tell a little about the story behind the hymn.

_____
_____
_____
_____
_____

TRUST AND OBEY

Text: John H. Sammis, 1887
Tune: Daniel B. Towner, 1887

1. When we walk with the Lord in the light of his word,
2. Not a bur - den we bear, not a sor - row we share,
3. But we ne - ver can prove the de - lights of his love
4. Then in fel - lows - hip sweet we will sit at his feet,

what a glo - ry he sheds on our way!
but our toil he doth rich - ly re - pay;
un - til all on the al - tar we lay;
or we'll walk by his side in the way;

While we do his good will, he a - bides with us still,
not a grief or a loss, not a frown or a cross,
for the fa - vor he shows, for the joy he bes - tows,
what he says we will do, where he sends we will go;

and with all who will trust and o - bey.
but is blest if we trust and o - bey.
are for them who will trust and o - bey.
ne - ver fear, on - ly trust and o - bey.

Refrain

Trust and o - bey, for there's no o - ther way to be

hap - py in Je - sus, but to trust and o - bey.

THINK ABOUT IT..

Read the verses of the hymn and match the themes with the correct verse.

Verse one   following God's call for our life

Verse two   during the difficult times in life

Verse three   our daily walk in life

Verse four   our total submission

Draw or write about a time in your life when it was hard to obey.

COPYWORK

Then in fellowship sweet

we will sit at his feet,

or we'll walk by his

side in the way; what he

says we will do, where

he sends we will go;

never fear, only trust

and obey.

Then in fellowship sweet
we will sit at his feet,
or we'll walk by his side in the way;
what he says we will do,
where he sends we will go;
never fear, only trust and obey.

Color the letters. Write words that describe how and why we obey all around the word "obey."

OBEDIENCE WORD SEARCH

```
Y P T U E Z Y I S Z N H S U M U U T X I
C N H O Y E S A H O Z P T A O T S U H W
F S L Y Z M I Z I J F G W J M H R B U O
B X Y N O L S T V D L Z E Y J X G U T Q
I U U E G N S V X O P R X B W X P T S L
B U U B J E Y X R C I F G R I M H K R T
D R L Z U P I Y Z X H V M J D G P L Q R
C I R Q R S Z Q Y H S J U V I T H P Q O
X Z B M M I B Y Q N W W B L E S S I N G
U O Y L E T E L P M O C E O P L Z S F P
X O I S F I O C G R L D E D P E J O R N
W I M M E D I A T E L Y W T T G N A I S
I N W W E Q K C W B E V E I L E B A W W
G K X O S Z Q H C C F W X Z T L I K K V
X K E V L I Z V Z Y W H P H O N O I T R
Q U J Y L H R N R Z W Z I V F X E G X E
V S D L O H R T M L G R E S Y U W S B B
X A Z A R W O G K H N E O M R D W N S F
F N S P D B S Y R C U P T E X O C W Z T
L G K K B I F T L Y W W P P G V O G E P
```

TRUST

LOVE

IMMEDIATELY

FELLOWSHIP

BELIEVE

BLESSING

QUESTION

LORD

GLORY

COMPLETELY

WITNESS

DELIGHT